EASY GUITAR
WITH NOTES & TAB

MW00804014

ISBN 978-1-4584-1370-3

Walt Disney Music Company
Wonderland Music Company, Inc.

DISTRIBUTED BY

HAL•LEONARD®
CORPORATION

7777 W. BLUEMOUND RD. P.O. BOX 13819 MILWAUKEE, WI 53213

In Australia contact:
Hal Leonard Australia Pty. Ltd.
4 Lentara Court
Cheltenham, Victoria, 3192 Australia
Email: ausadmin@halleonard.com.au

Visit Hal Leonard Online at
www.halleonard.com

CONTENTS

STRUM AND PICK PATTERNS

This chart contains the suggested strum and pick patterns that are referred to by number at the beginning of each song in this book. The symbols ⊓ and ∨ in the strum patterns refer to down and up strokes, respectively. The letters in the pick patterns indicate which right-hand fingers play which strings.

p = thumb
i = index finger
m = middle finger
a = ring finger

For example; Pick Pattern 2
is played: thumb - index - middle - ring

Strum Patterns   Pick Patterns

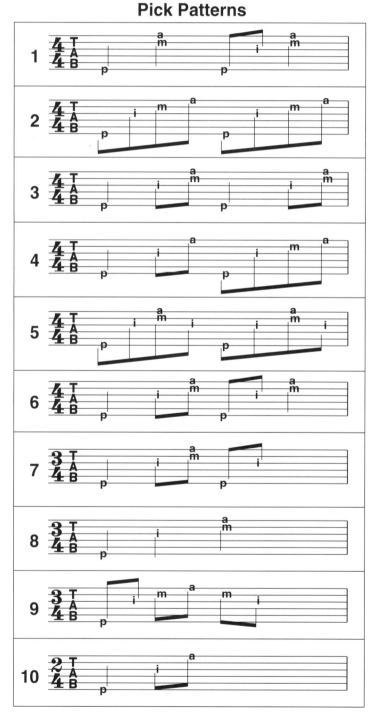

You can use the 3/4 Strum and Pick Patterns in songs written in compound meter (6/8, 9/8, 12/8, etc.).
For example, you can accompany a song in 6/8 by playing the 3/4 pattern twice in each measure.
The 4/4 Strum and Pick Patterns can be used for songs written in cut time (¢) by doubling the note time values in the patterns. Each pattern would therefore last two measures in cut time.

The Black Pearl

from Walt Disney Pictures' PIRATES OF THE CARIBBEAN: THE CURSE OF THE BLACK PEARL

Music by Klaus Badelt

Strum Pattern: 8
Pick Pattern: 8

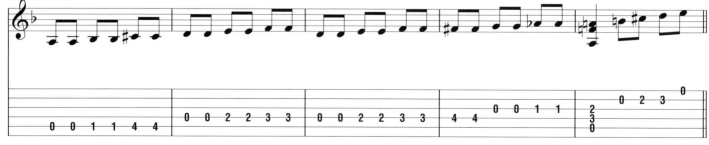

Angelica

from Walt Disney Pictures' PIRATES OF THE CARIBBEAN: ON STRANGER TIDES

Music by Hans Zimmer, Eduardo Cruz, Rodrigo Sanchez and Gabriela Quintero

Strum Pattern: 4
Pick Pattern: 3

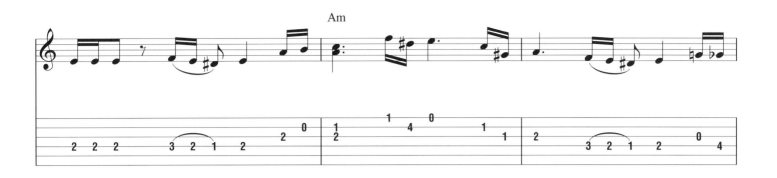

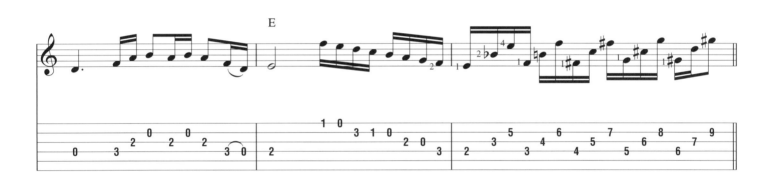

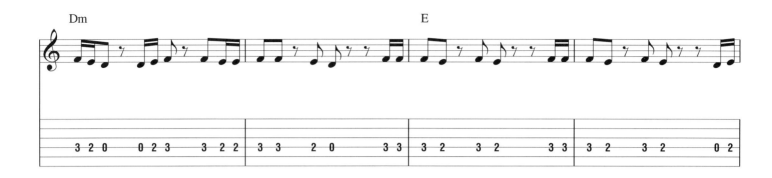

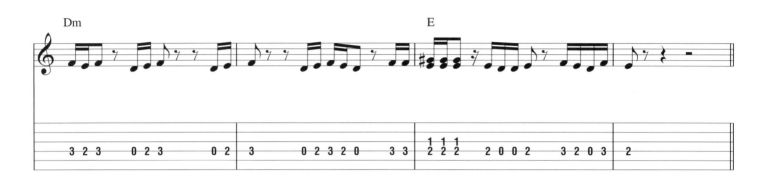

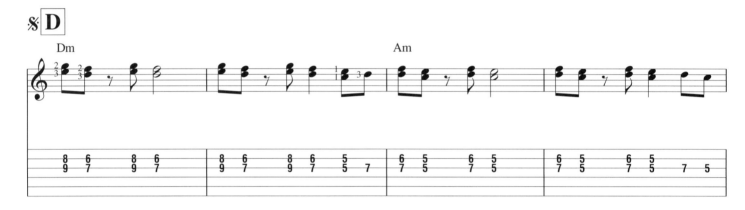

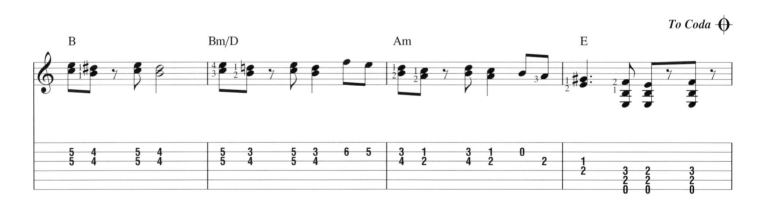

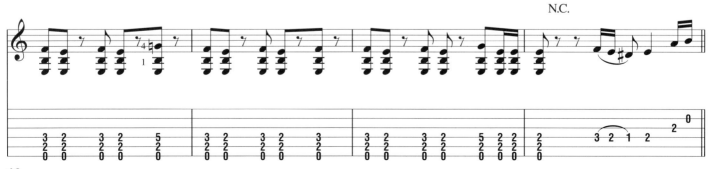

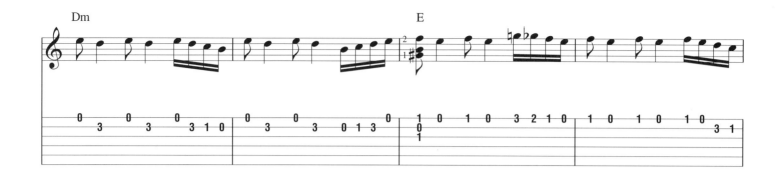

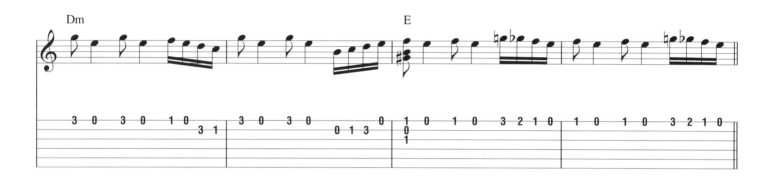

G

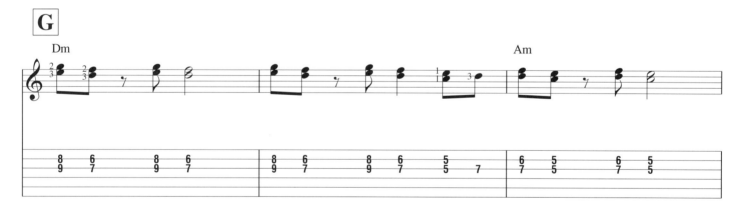

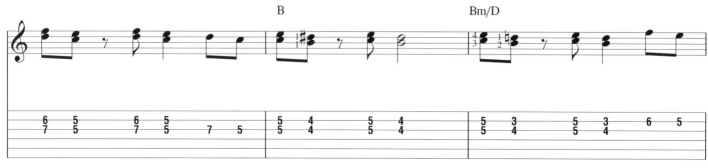

Blood Ritual

from Walt Disney Pictures' PIRATES OF THE CARIBBEAN: THE CURSE OF THE BLACK PEARL

Music by Klaus Badelt

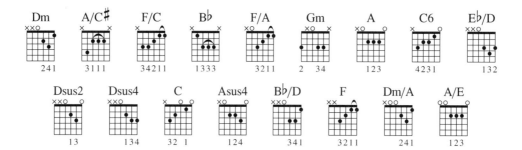

Strum Pattern: 3
Pick Pattern: 3

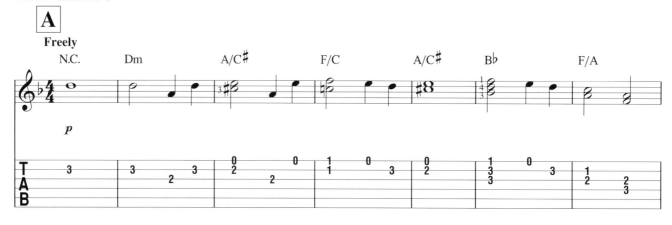

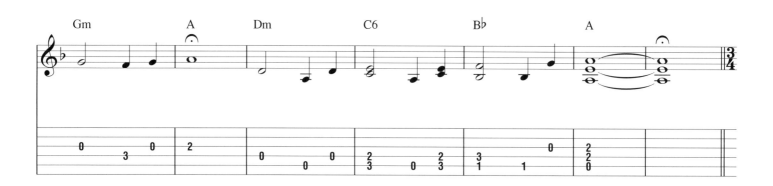

*Use Pattern 9 for meas.

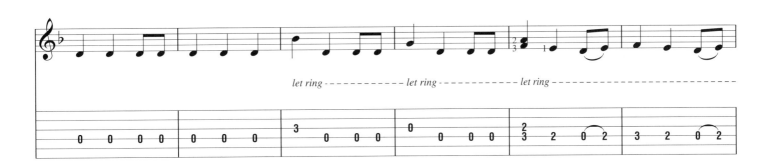

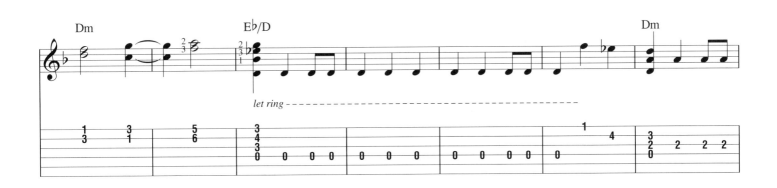

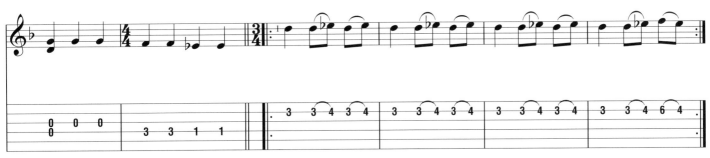

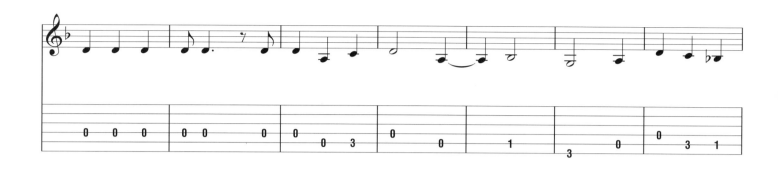

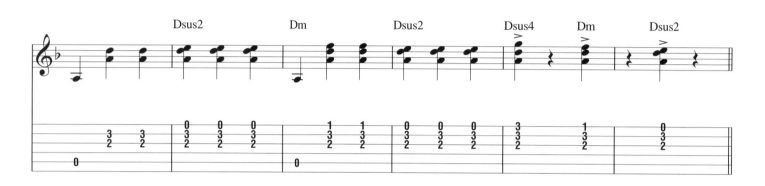

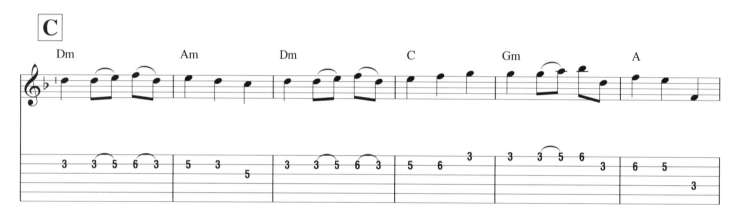

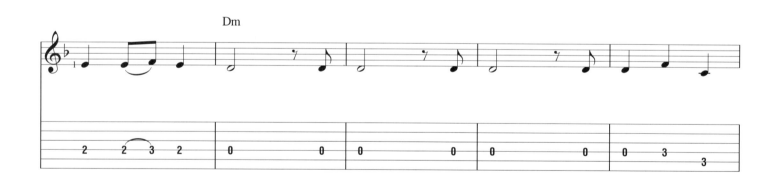

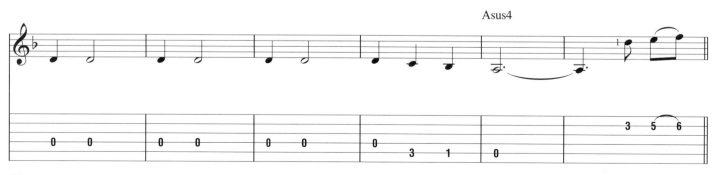

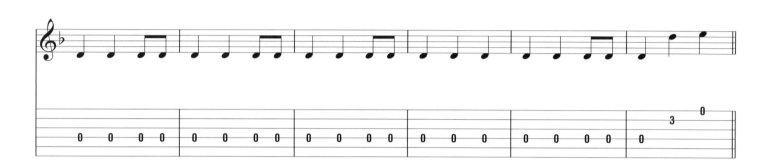

F

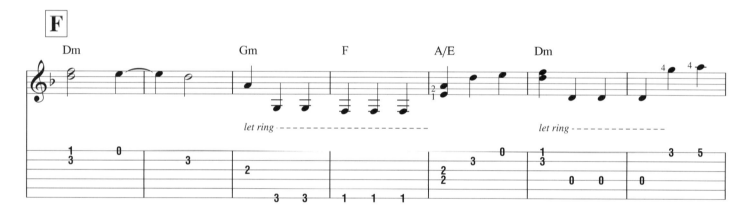

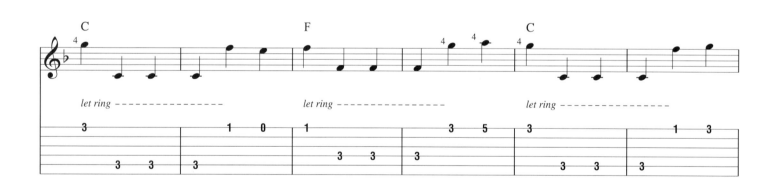

Davy Jones

from Walt Disney Pictures' PIRATES OF THE CARIBBEAN: DEAD MAN'S CHEST

Music by Hans Zimmer

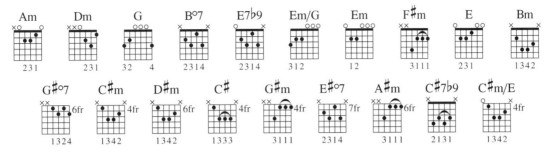

*Capo V

Strum Pattern: 8
Pick Pattern: 8

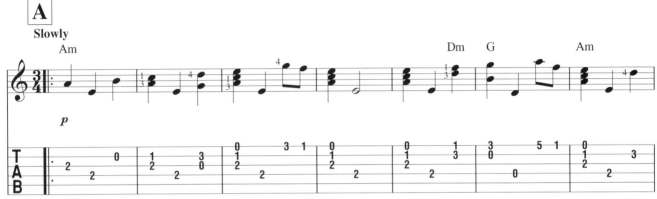

*Optional: To match recording, place capo at 5th fret

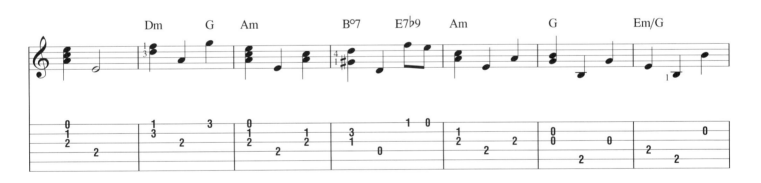

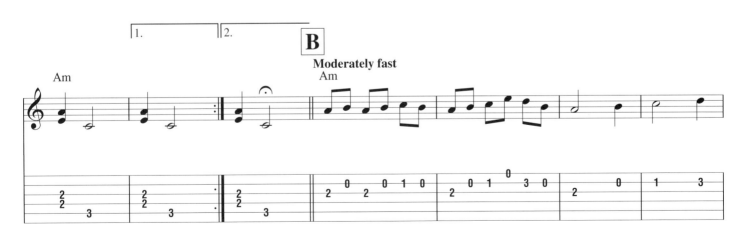

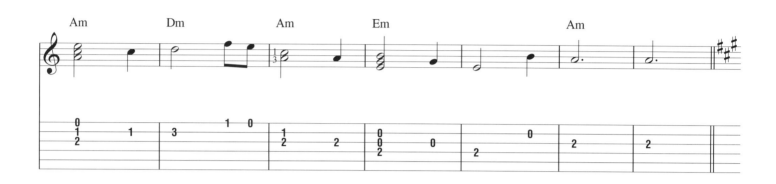

He's a Pirate

from Walt Disney Pictures' PIRATES OF THE CARIBBEAN: THE CURSE OF THE BLACK PEARL

Music by Klaus Badelt

*Optional: To match recording, place capo at 5th fret.

Hoist the Colours

from Walt Disney Pictures' PIRATES OF THE CARIBBEAN: AT WORLD'S END

Lyrics by Ted Elliot and Terry Rossio
Music by Hans Zimmer and Gore Verbinski

I've Got My Eye on You

from Walt Disney Pictures' PIRATES OF THE CARIBBEAN: DEAD MAN'S CHEST

Music by Hans Zimmer

Strum Pattern: 8
Pick Pattern: 8

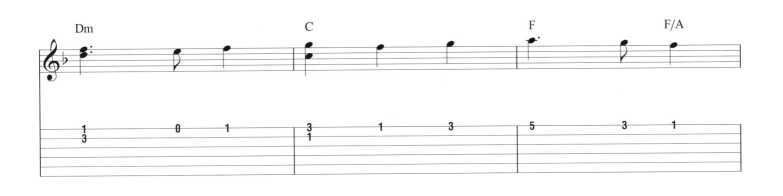

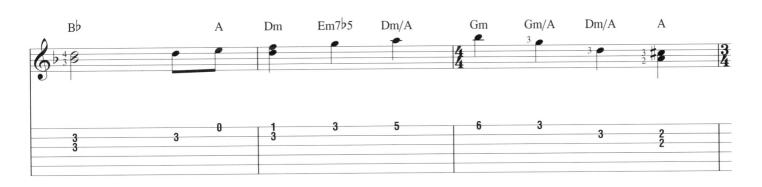

The Kraken

from Walt Disney Pictures' PIRATES OF THE CARIBBEAN: DEAD MAN'S CHEST

Music by Hans Zimmer

Strum Pattern: 1, 5
Pick Pattern: 5

*Use Pattern 7 for meas.

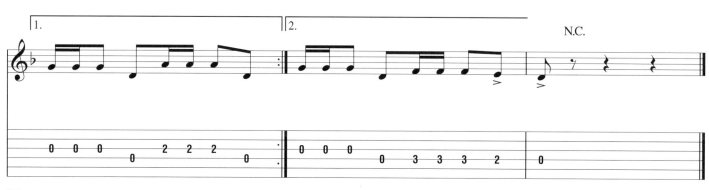

The Medallion Calls

from Walt Disney Pictures' PIRATES OF THE CARIBBEAN: THE CURSE OF THE BLACK PEARL

Music by Klaus Badelt

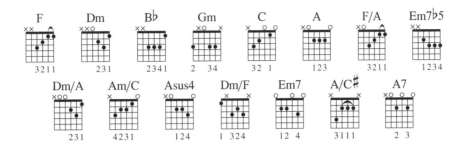

*Strum Pattern: 3
*Pick Pattern: 3

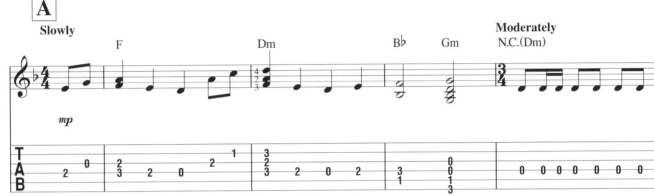

*Use Pattern 8 for   meas.

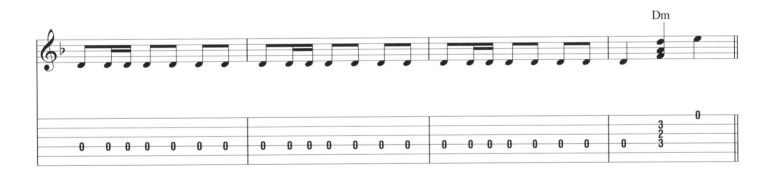

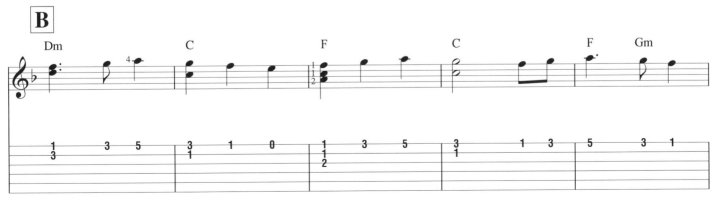

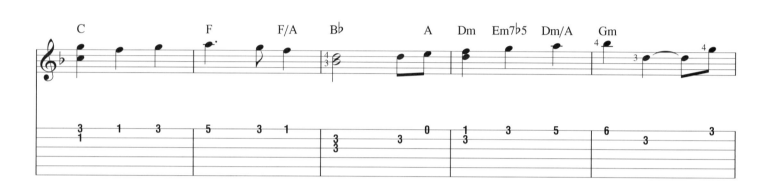

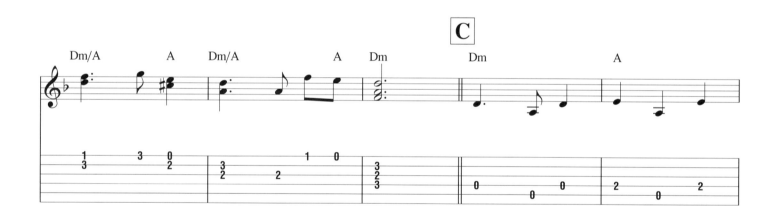

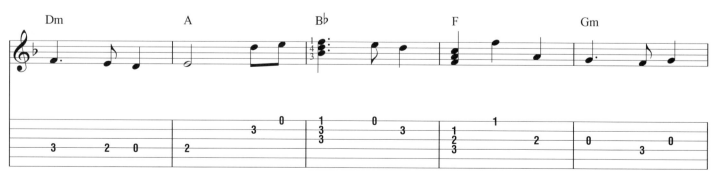

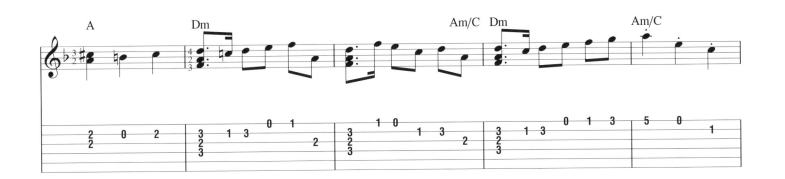

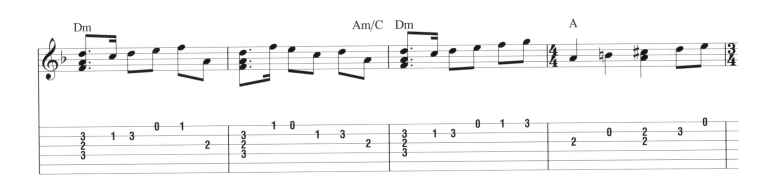

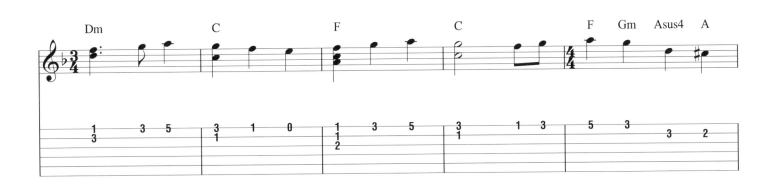

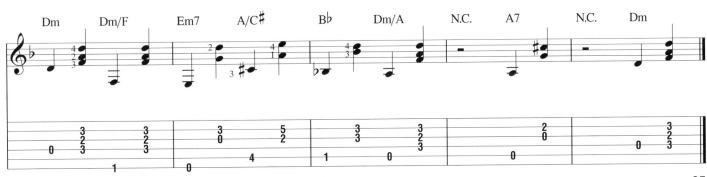

Mermaids

from Walt Disney Pictures' PIRATES OF THE CARIBBEAN: ON STRANGER TIDES
Music by Hans Zimmer and Eric Whitacre

Strum Pattern: 9
Pick Pattern: 9

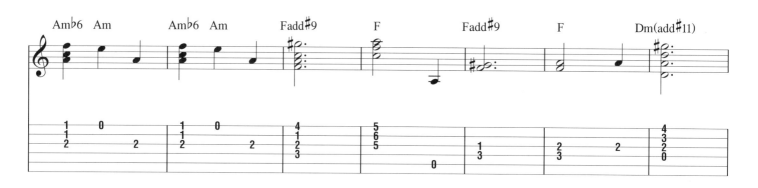

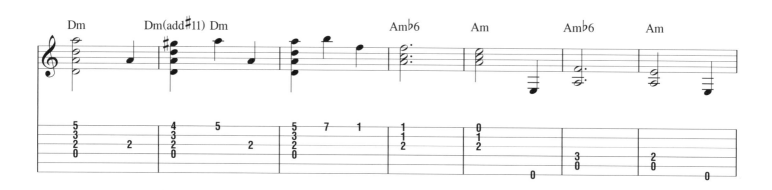

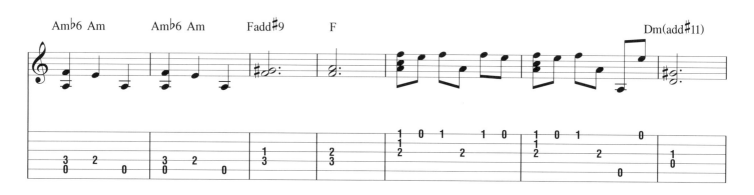

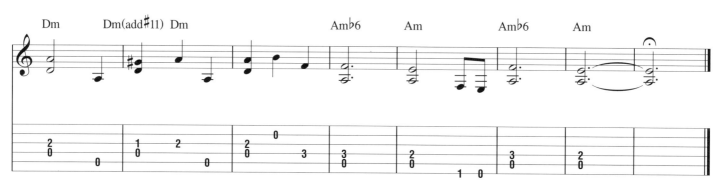

Up Is Down

from Walt Disney Pictures' PIRATES OF THE CARIBBEAN: AT WORLD'S END
Music by Hans Zimmer

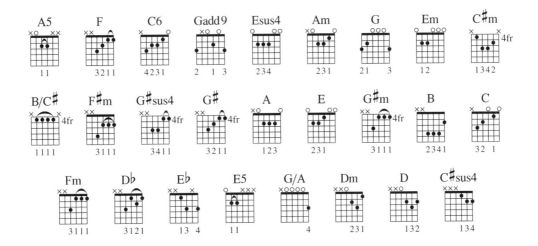

*Capo V

Strum Pattern: 8
Pick Pattern: 8

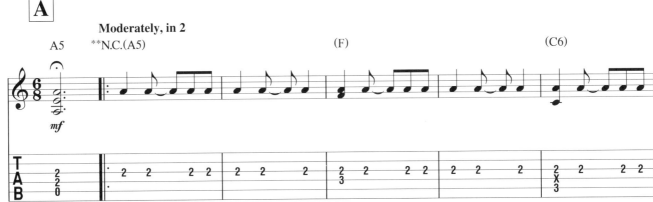

*Optional: To match recording, place capo at 5th fret.
**Chord symbols in parentheses reflect implied harmony.

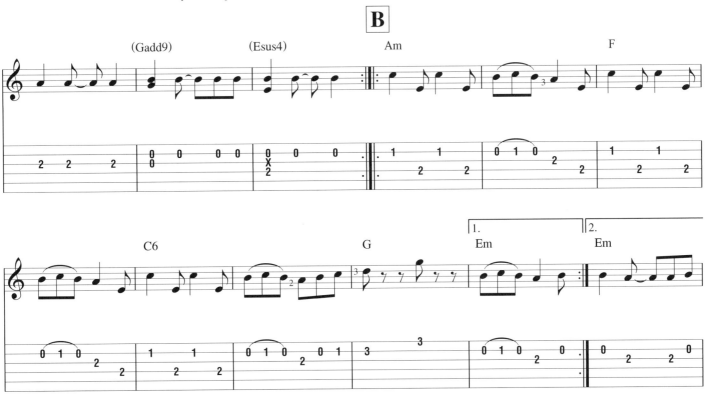

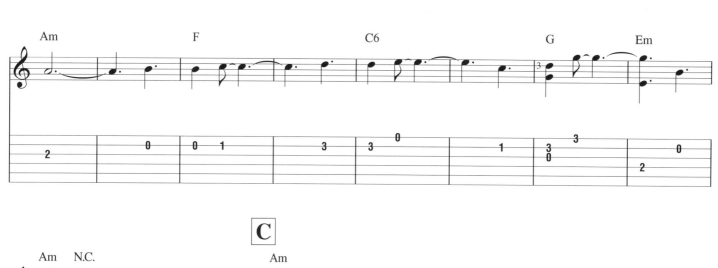

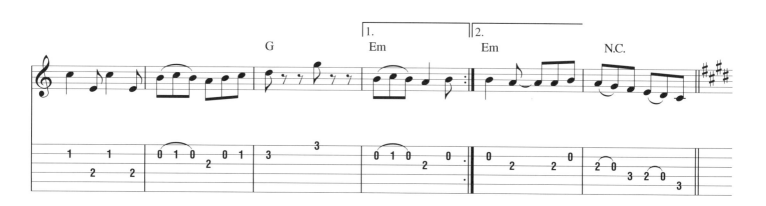

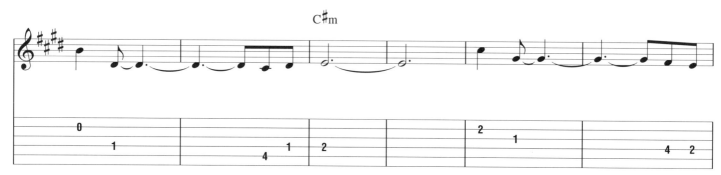

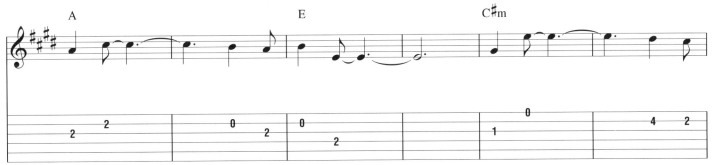

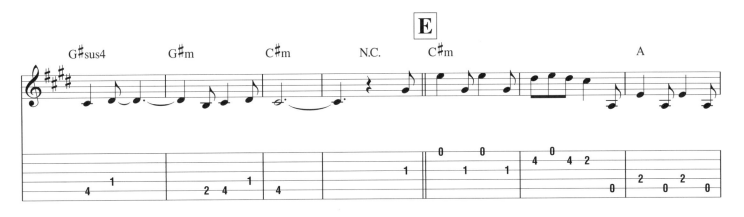

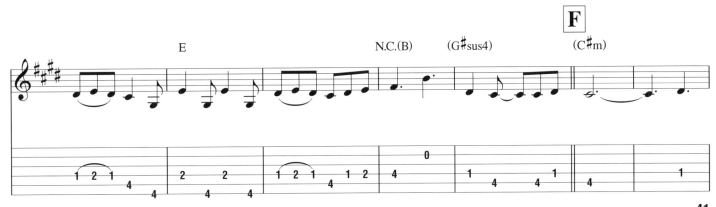

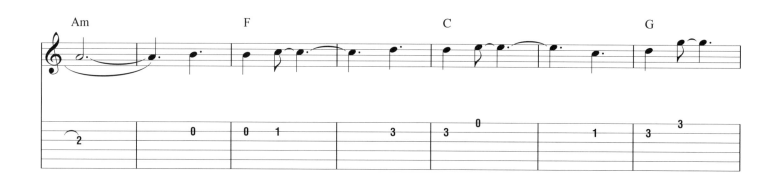

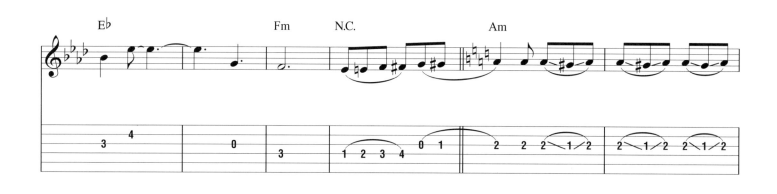
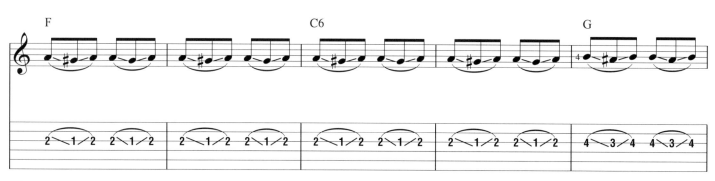

Moonlight Serenade

from Walt Disney Pictures' PIRATES OF THE CARIBBEAN: THE CURSE OF THE BLACK PEARL

Music by Klaus Badelt

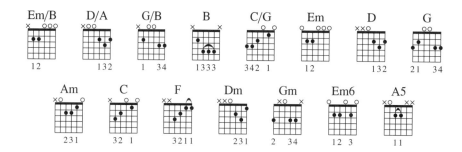

*Capo V

Strum Pattern: 3
Pick Pattern: 3

A Moderately

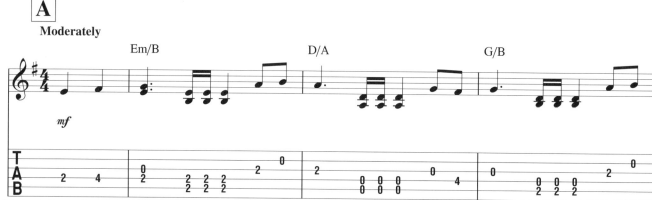

mf

*Optional: To match recording, place capo at 5th fret.

**Use Pattern 8 for   and   meas.

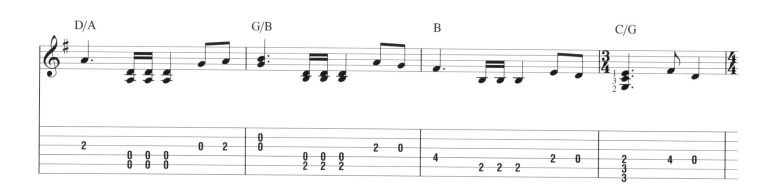

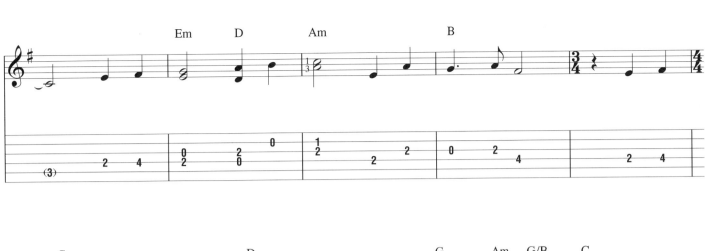

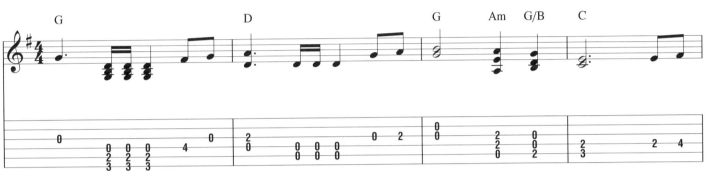

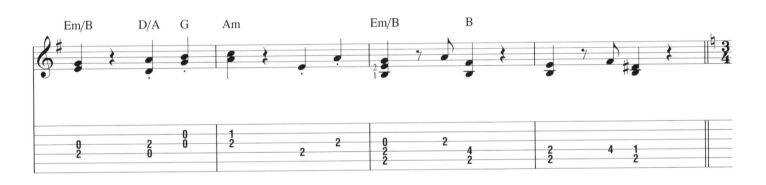

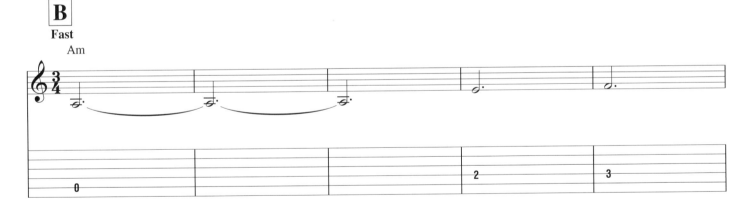

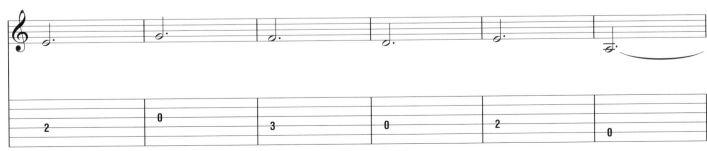

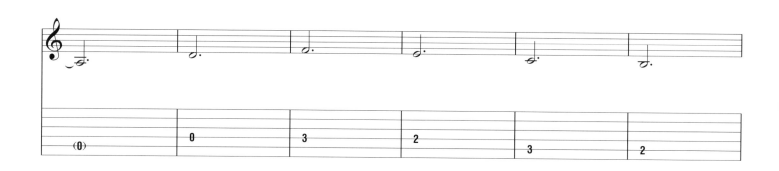

Em

C

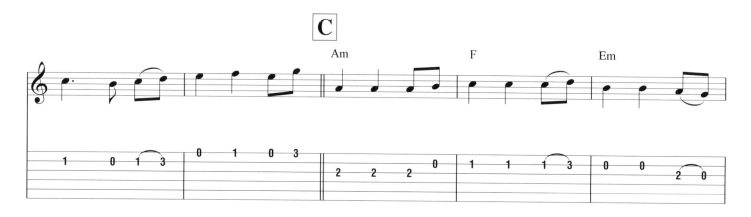

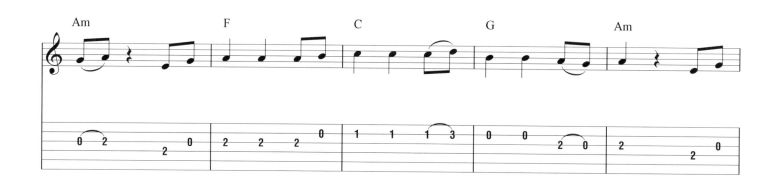

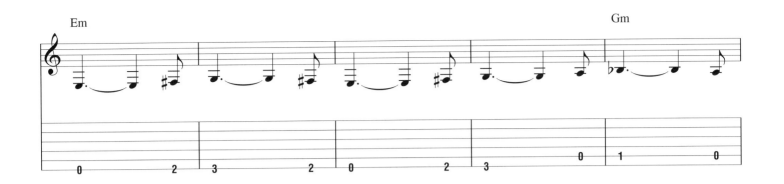

D

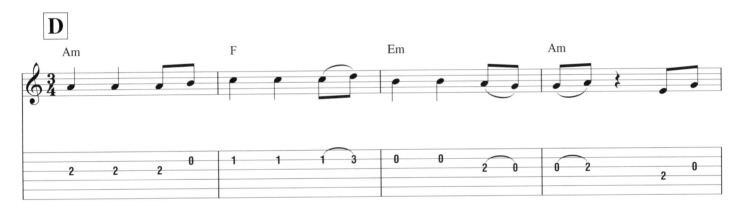

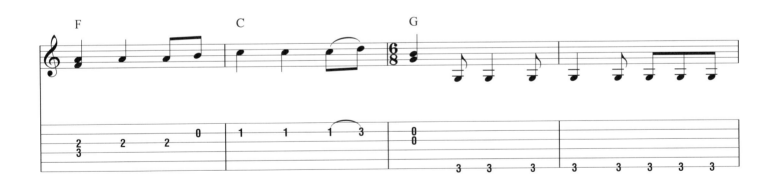

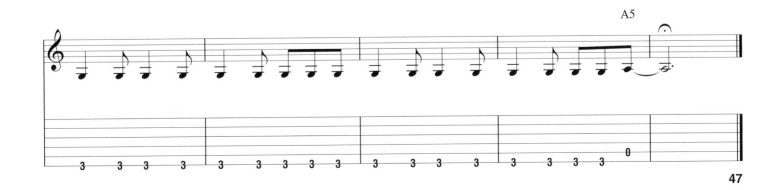

One Day

from Walt Disney Pictures' PIRATES OF THE CARIBBEAN: AT WORLD'S END
Music by Hans Zimmer

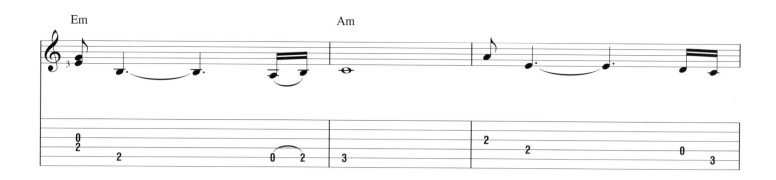

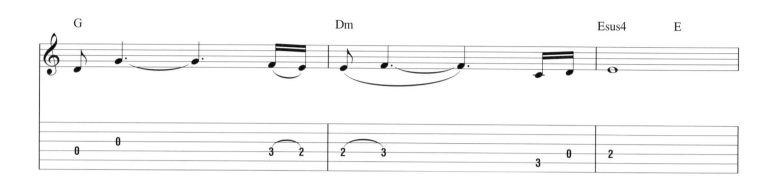

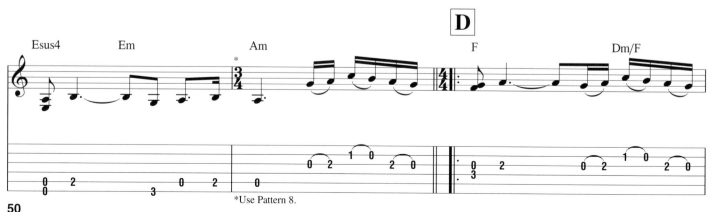

*Use Pattern 8.

50

Two Hornpipes
(Fisher's Hornpipe)

from Walt Disney Pictures' PIRATES OF THE CARIBBEAN: DEAD MAN'S CHEST
By Skip Henderson

*Optional: To match recording, place capo at 2nd fret.

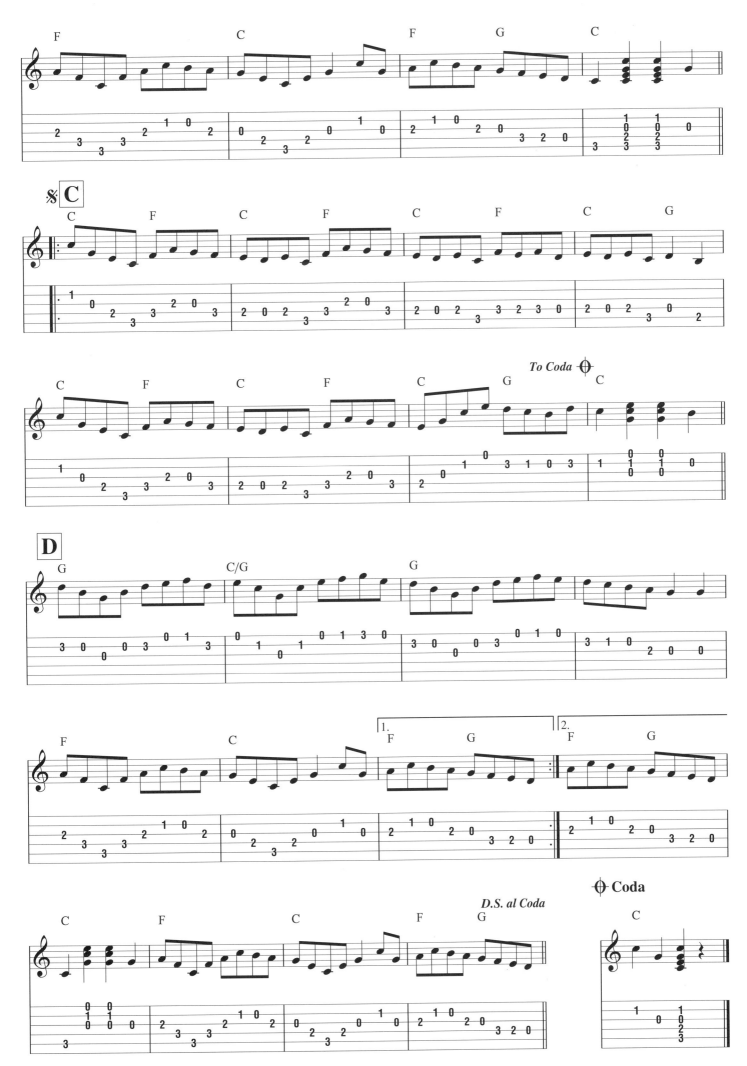

Hal•Leonard GUITAR PLAY-ALONG

This series will help you play your favorite songs quickly and easily. Just follow the tab and listen to the CD to hear how the guitar should sound, and then play along using the separate backing tracks. Mac or PC users can also slow down the tempo without changing pitch by using the CD in their computer. The melody and lyrics are included in the book so that you can sing or simply follow along.

61. SLIPKNOT
00699775......................$14.95

62. CHRISTMAS CAROLS
00699798......................$12.95

63. CREEDENCE CLEARWATER REVIVAL
00699802......................$16.99

64. OZZY OSBOURNE
00699803......................$16.99

65. THE DOORS
00699806......................$16.99

66. THE ROLLING STONES
00699807......................$16.95

67. BLACK SABBATH
00699808......................$16.99

**68. PINK FLOYD –
DARK SIDE OF THE MOON**
00699809......................$16.99

69. ACOUSTIC FAVORITES
00699810......................$14.95

70. OZZY OSBOURNE
00699805......................$16.99

71. CHRISTIAN ROCK
00699824......................$14.95

72. ACOUSTIC '90s
00699827......................$14.95

73. BLUESY ROCK
00699829......................$16.99

74. PAUL BALOCHE
00699831......................$14.95

75. TOM PETTY
00699882......................$16.99

76. COUNTRY HITS
00699884......................$14.95

77. BLUEGRASS
00699910......................$12.99

78. NIRVANA
00700132......................$16.99

88. ACOUSTIC ANTHOLOGY
00700175......................$19.95

81. ROCK ANTHOLOGY
00700176......................$22.99

82. EASY ROCK SONGS
00700177......................$12.99

83. THREE CHORD SONGS
00700178......................$16.99

84. STEELY DAN
00700200......................$16.99

85. THE POLICE
00700269......................$16.99

86. BOSTON
00700465......................$16.99

87. ACOUSTIC WOMEN
00700763......................$14.99

88. GRUNGE
00700467......................$16.99

91. BLUES INSTRUMENTALS
00700505......................$14.99

**92. EARLY ROCK
INSTRUMENTALS**
00700506......................$12.99

93. ROCK INSTRUMENTALS
00700507......................$16.99

96. THIRD DAY
00700560......................$14.95

97. ROCK BAND
00700703......................$14.99

98. ROCK BAND
00700704......................$14.95

99. ZZ TOP
00700762......................$16.99

100. B.B. KING
00700466......................$14.99

102. CLASSIC PUNK
00700769......................$14.99

103. SWITCHFOOT
00700773......................$16.99

104. DUANE ALLMAN
00700846......................$16.99

106. WEEZER
00700958......................$14.99

107. CREAM
00701069......................$16.99

108. THE WHO
00701053......................$16.99

109. STEVE MILLER
00701054......................$14.99

111. JOHN MELLENCAMP
00701056......................$14.99

113. JIM CROCE
00701058......................$14.99

114. BON JOVI
00701060......................$14.99

115. JOHNNY CASH
00701070......................$16.99

116. THE VENTURES
00701124......................$14.99

119. AC/DC CLASSICS
00701356......................$17.99

120. PROGRESSIVE ROCK
00701457......................$14.99

122. CROSBY, STILLS & NASH
00701610......................$16.99

**123. LENNON & McCARTNEY
ACOUSTIC**
00701614......................$16.99

124. MODERN WORSHIP
00701629......................$14.99

126. BOB MARLEY
00701701......................$16.99

127. 1970s ROCK
00701739......................$14.99

128. 1960s ROCK
00701740......................$14.99

129. MEGADETH
00701741......................$14.99

130. IRON MAIDEN
00701742......................$14.99

131. 1990s ROCK
00701743......................$14.99

133. TAYLOR SWIFT
00701894......................$16.99

0311

EASY GUITAR
WITH NOTES & TAB

This series features simplified arrangements with notes, tab, chord charts, and strum and pick patterns.

Prices, contents and availability subject to change without notice.

FOR MORE INFORMATION,
SEE YOUR LOCAL MUSIC DEALER,
OR WRITE TO:

HAL•LEONARD®
CORPORATION
7777 W. BLUEMOUND RD. P.O. BOX 13819
MILWAUKEE, WISCONSIN 53213
Visit Hal Leonard online at
www.halleonard.com

MIXED FOLIOS

00702287	Acoustic	$14.99
00702002	Acoustic Rock Hits for Easy Guitar	$12.95
00702166	All-Time Best Guitar Collection	$19.99
00699665	Beatles Best	$12.95
00702232	Best Acoustic Songs for Easy Guitar	$12.99
00702233	Best Hard Rock Songs	$14.99
00698978	Big Christmas Collection	$16.95
00702115	Blues Classics	$10.95
00385020	Broadway Songs for Kids	$9.95
00702237	Christian Acoustic Favorites	$12.95
00702149	Children's Christian Songbook	$7.95
00702028	Christmas Classics	$7.95
00702185	Christmas Hits	$9.95
00702016	Classic Blues for Easy Guitar	$12.95
00702141	Classic Rock	$8.95
00702203	CMT's 100 Greatest Country Songs	$27.95
00702170	Contemporary Christian Christmas	$9.95
00702006	Contemporary Christian Favorites	$9.95
00702065	Contemporary Women of Country	$9.95
00702239	Country Classics for Easy Guitar	$19.99
00702282	Country Hits of 2009-2010	$14.99
00702240	Country Hits of 2007-2008	$12.95
00702225	Country Hits of '06-'07	$12.95
00702085	Disney Movie Hits	$12.95
00702257	Easy Acoustic Guitar Songs	$14.99
00702280	Easy Guitar Tab White Pages	$29.99
00702212	Essential Christmas	$9.95
00702041	Favorite Hymns for Easy Guitar	$9.95
00702281	4 Chord Rock	$9.99
00702286	Glee	$16.99
00702174	God Bless America® & Other Songs for a Better Nation	$8.95
00699374	Gospel Favorites	$14.95
00702160	The Great American Country Songbook	$14.95
00702050	Great Classical Themes for Easy Guitar	$6.95
00702131	Great Country Hits of the '90s	$8.95
00702116	Greatest Hymns for Guitar	$8.95
00702130	The Groovy Years	$9.95
00702184	Guitar Instrumentals	$9.95
00702231	High School Musical for Easy Guitar	$12.95
00702241	High School Musical 2	$12.95
00702046	Hits of the '70s for Easy Guitar	$8.95
00702032	International Songs for Easy Guitar	$12.95
00702275	Jazz Favorites for Easy Guitar	$14.99
00702051	Jock Rock for Easy Guitar	$9.95
00702162	Jumbo Easy Guitar Songbook	$19.95
00702112	Latin Favorites	$9.95
00702258	Legends of Rock	$14.99
00702138	Mellow Rock Hits	$10.95
00702261	Modern Worship Hits	$14.99
00702147	Motown's Greatest Hits	$9.95
00702189	MTV's 100 Greatest Pop Songs	$24.95
00702272	1950s Rock	$14.99
00702271	1960s Rock	$14.99
00702270	1970s Rock	$14.99
00702269	1980s Rock	$14.99
00702268	1990s Rock	$14.99
00702187	Selections from O Brother Where Art Thou?	$12.95
00702178	100 Songs for Kids	$12.95
00702125	Praise and Worship for Guitar	$9.95
00702155	Rock Hits for Guitar	$9.95
00702242	Rock Band	$19.95
00702256	Rock Band 2	$19.95
00702128	Rockin' Down the Highway	$9.95
00702110	The Sound of Music	$9.99
00702285	Southern Rock Hits	$12.99
00702124	Today's Christian Rock – 2nd Edition	$9.95
00702220	Today's Country Hits	$9.95
00702198	Today's Hits for Guitar	$9.95
00702217	Top Christian Hits	$12.95
00702235	Top Christian Hits of '07-'08	$14.95
00702284	Top Hits of 2010	$14.99
00702246	Top Hits of 2008	$12.95
00702206	Very Best of Rock	$9.95
00702255	VH1's 100 Greatest Hard Rock Songs	$27.95
00702175	VH1's 100 Greatest Songs of Rock and Roll	$24.95
00702253	Wicked	$12.99
00702192	Worship Favorites	$9.95

ARTIST COLLECTIONS

00702267	AC/DC for Easy Guitar	$14.99
00702001	Best of Aerosmith	$16.95
00702040	Best of the Allman Brothers	$14.99
00702169	Best of The Beach Boys	$10.95
00702201	The Essential Black Sabbath	$12.95
00702140	Best of Brooks & Dunn	$10.95
00702095	Best of Mariah Carey	$12.95
00702043	Best of Johnny Cash	$14.99
00702033	Best of Steven Curtis Chapman	$14.95
00702263	Best of Casting Crowns	$12.99
00702090	Eric Clapton's Best	$10.95
00702086	Eric Clapton – from the Album Unplugged	$10.95
00702202	The Essential Eric Clapton	$12.95
00702250	blink-182 – Greatest Hits	$12.99
00702053	Best of Patsy Cline	$10.95
00702229	The Very Best of Creedence Clearwater Revival	$12.95
00702145	Best of Jim Croce	$10.95
00702278	Crosby, Stills & Nash	$12.99
00702219	David Crowder*Band Collection	$12.95
00702122	The Doors for Easy Guitar	$12.99
00702276	Fleetwood Mac – Easy Guitar Collection	$12.99
00702099	Best of Amy Grant	$9.95
00702190	Best of Pat Green	$19.95
00702136	Best of Merle Haggard	$12.99
00702243	Hannah Montana	$14.95
00702244	Hannah Montana 2/Meet Miley Cyrus	$16.95
00702227	Jimi Hendrix – Smash Hits	$14.99
00702236	Best of Antonio Carlos Jobim	$12.95
00702087	Best of Billy Joel	$10.95
00702245	Elton John – Greatest Hits 1970-2002	$14.99
00702204	Robert Johnson	$9.95
00702277	Best of Jonas Brothers	$14.99
00702234	Selections from Toby Keith – 35 Biggest Hits	$12.95
00702003	Kiss	$9.95
00702193	Best of Jennifer Knapp	$12.95
00702097	John Lennon – Imagine	$9.95
00702216	Lynyrd Skynyrd	$15.99
00702182	The Essential Bob Marley	$12.95
00702248	Paul McCartney – All the Best	$14.99
00702129	Songs of Sarah McLachlan	$12.95
02501316	Metallica – Death Magnetic	$15.95
00702209	Steve Miller Band – Young Hearts (Greatest Hits)	$12.95
00702096	Best of Nirvana	$14.95
00702211	The Offspring – Greatest Hits	$12.95
00702030	Best of Roy Orbison	$12.95
00702144	Best of Ozzy Osbourne	$12.95
00702279	Tom Petty	$12.99
00702139	Elvis Country Favorites	$9.95
00699415	Best of Queen for Guitar	$14.99
00702208	Red Hot Chili Peppers – Greatest Hits	$12.95
00702093	Rolling Stones Collection	$17.95
00702092	Best of the Rolling Stones	$14.99
00702196	Best of Bob Seger	$12.95
00702252	Frank Sinatra – Nothing But the Best	$12.99
00702010	Best of Rod Stewart	$14.95
00702150	Best of Sting	$12.95
00702049	Best of George Strait	$12.95
00702259	Taylor Swift for Easy Guitar	$12.99
00702290	Taylor Swift – Speak Now	$12.99
00702223	Chris Tomlin – Arriving	$12.95
00702262	Chris Tomlin Collection	$14.99
00702226	Chris Tomlin – See the Morning	$12.95
00702132	Shania Twain – Greatest Hits	$10.95
00702108	Best of Stevie Ray Vaughan	$10.95
00702123	Best of Hank Williams	$12.99
00702111	Stevie Wonder – Guitar Collection	$9.95
00702228	Neil Young – Greatest Hits	$12.99
00702188	Essential ZZ Top	$10.95

0211